Das Große Ballonabenteuer: Zweisprachige Englisch-Deutsche Geschichten

My Pommeline

Published by My Pommeline, 2024.

DAS GROSSE BALLONABENTEUER: ZWEISPRACHIGE ENGLISCH-DEUTSCHE GESCHICHTEN

First edition. October 27, 2024.

Copyright © 2024 My Pommeline.

ISBN: 979-8227289506

Written by My Pommeline.

Table of Contents

The Giant with the Little Garden

Once upon a time, in a land where the hills rolled for miles and the rivers snaked through valleys like silver ribbons, there lived a giant. He was a big, burly, and very grumpy giant named Grumbleton. The kingdom he ruled over was as barren as his heart—dry, grey, and utterly lifeless. Not a single flower bloomed, and not even the birds dared to sing. Grumbleton liked it that way, or so he thought.

Each morning, the giant would stomp across his land, his massive boots thudding against the hard ground. The sound echoed through the hills, sending what few creatures there were scurrying for cover. "Bah! Another dull day," Grumbleton would grumble to himself. "No noisy birds, no pesky flowers. Just how I like it."

But one day, something unexpected happened. As Grumbleton was wandering his usual path, he noticed a splash of color out of the corner of his eye. At first, he thought it was a trick of the sunlight. He squinted, then bent down, his enormous hands resting on his knees. And there, nestled between two jagged rocks, was the tiniest, most beautiful little garden he had ever seen.

The garden was no bigger than one of Grumbleton's hands, but it was bursting with life. Bright yellow daffodils swayed gently in the breeze, deep red roses bloomed, and delicate bluebells nodded their heads. There was even a small pond with a shimmering surface, reflecting the vivid colors of the flowers. Butterflies flitted about, bees buzzed busily, and a tiny bird was chirping a cheerful song.

Grumbleton frowned. He didn't like things that were cheerful.

"Who put this here?" he muttered. "In my kingdom? Without my permission?" He stomped his foot, and the ground trembled. But the garden didn't wither or disappear. It stood there, quietly blooming, as if to defy his grumpiness.

"I suppose I could destroy it," Grumbleton growled. He reached out to pluck one of the roses, but as soon as his thick fingers touched the delicate petals, the stem pricked him with a thorn.

"Ow!" he yelped, pulling back his hand. The thorn was tiny, barely noticeable, but it hurt more than it should have. Grumbleton scowled and rubbed his finger. "Stupid garden."

The giant turned to leave, but something stopped him. Despite himself, Grumbleton was curious. How had this tiny garden survived in his kingdom of dust and rock? Who had cared for it? Why was it here?

For the next few days, Grumbleton kept coming back to the little garden, each time with a new plan to rid himself of it. First, he tried stamping on the rocks around it, but his feet were too big, and he nearly tripped. Then he tried pulling up the flowers by their roots, but they slipped through his fingers like sand. He even tried watering it too much, thinking it might drown. But instead, the garden flourished. The flowers bloomed even brighter, and the little bird sang louder than ever.

Frustrated, Grumbleton sat down with a huff. "Why won't you go away?" he grumbled at the garden. "What's so special about you?"

To his surprise, a tiny voice answered. "Perhaps it's not what's special about the garden," said the voice. "But what it can teach you."

Grumbleton looked around in confusion, then spotted a small, delicate butterfly perched on a nearby daffodil. It flapped its wings lazily and spoke again. "You've been rough and grumpy with us, Giant. Gardens need care, patience, and kindness to grow."

"Care? Patience? Bah!" Grumbleton scoffed. "I'm a giant! I don't have time for silly things like that."

"But you do have time to destroy things, don't you?" the butterfly asked, fluttering closer to Grumbleton's face. "Why not try the opposite for once? Try helping the garden grow instead."

Grumbleton was about to argue, but he paused. He was a giant—strong and powerful—but all his efforts to destroy the garden had failed. What if he tried something different?

The next day, Grumbleton returned to the little garden, but this time, he didn't stomp or grumble. He crouched down as carefully as he could and gently touched the leaves. He tried to water it, but not too much. And though it was awkward for a giant of his size, he used his giant fingers to clear away weeds.

At first, it was hard. Grumbleton's hands were big and clumsy, and he accidentally squashed a few flowers. He knocked over the tiny bird's nest more than once. But something amazing happened: the more careful and patient he was, the more the garden grew.

Soon, the little garden wasn't so little anymore. It spread out, winding through the rocks and cracks, turning the grey, barren land into a sea of color. Flowers of all kinds sprouted, trees began to grow, and birds from far and wide came to sing. Grumbleton's kingdom was no longer a place of dullness and dust, but one of life and beauty.

As the garden grew, so did Grumbleton's heart. He found that caring for something so small and fragile made him feel lighter, happier. The creatures of the garden—bees, butterflies, and birds—became his friends, and soon the once grumpy giant was smiling. He even began to hum a little tune as he worked.

One day, as Grumbleton admired the now sprawling garden, the tiny bird landed on his shoulder. "You see?" it chirped. "You didn't need strength to make your kingdom beautiful. Just a little patience and kindness."

Grumbleton smiled, a warm and genuine smile. "I suppose I learned something after all," he said softly. "Even giants have a little room for magic."

And from that day on, the garden became the heart of Grumbleton's kingdom. Travelers from far and wide came to see the miraculous garden of the once-grumpy giant, and Grumbleton welcomed them all with a smile. His kingdom was no longer barren, but a place where life bloomed—thanks to a little garden, a lot of patience, and the kindness of a giant who learned to care.

Der Riese mit dem kleinen Garten

Es war einmal, in einem Land, wo die Hügel sich meilenweit erstreckten und die Flüsse wie silberne Bänder durch die Täler schlängelten, lebte ein Riese. Er war ein großer, kräftiger und sehr grimmiger Riese namens Grummelton. Das Königreich, über das er herrschte, war so karg wie sein Herz – trocken, grau und völlig leblos. Keine einzige Blume blühte, und nicht einmal die Vögel wagten es zu singen. Grummelton gefiel das so, oder zumindest dachte er das.

Jeden Morgen stampfte der Riese über sein Land, seine massiven Stiefel donnerten gegen den harten Boden. Der Klang hallte durch die Hügel und ließ die wenigen Kreaturen, die es gab, sich in Deckung flüchten. „Bah! Ein weiterer langweiliger Tag," murmelte Grummelton vor sich hin. „Keine lärmenden Vögel, keine lästigen Blumen. Genau so mag ich es."

Doch eines Tages passierte etwas Unerwartetes. Als Grummelton seinen gewohnten Weg wanderte, bemerkte er aus dem Augenwinkel einen Farbtupfer. Zunächst dachte er, es sei ein Lichtspiel der Sonne. Er blinzelte, beugte sich dann hinunter, seine riesigen Hände ruhten auf seinen Knien. Und dort, eingequetscht zwischen zwei scharfen Felsen, befand sich der winzigste, schönste kleine Garten, den er je gesehen hatte.

Der Garten war nicht größer als eine von Grummeltons Händen, aber er war voller Leben. Helle gelbe Narzissen wiegten sich sanft im Wind, tiefrote Rosen blühten, und zarte

Glockenblumen nickten mit ihren Köpfen. Es gab sogar einen kleinen Teich mit einer schimmernden Oberfläche, die die lebhaften Farben der Blumen widerspiegelte. Schmetterlinge schwirrten umher, Bienen summten fleißig, und ein kleiner Vogel zwitscherte ein fröhliches Lied.

Grummelton runzelte die Stirn. Er mochte keine fröhlichen Dinge.

„Wer hat das hier hergebracht?" murmelte er. „In meinem Königreich? Ohne meine Erlaubnis?" Er stampfte mit dem Fuß, und der Boden bebte. Aber der Garten welkte nicht und verschwand nicht. Er stand da, blühte still vor sich hin, als wolle er seine Griesgrämigkeit herausfordern.

„Ich könnte ihn wohl zerstören," knurrte Grummelton. Er streckte die Hand aus, um eine der Rosen zu pflücken, aber sobald seine dicken Finger die zarten Blütenblätter berührten, stach ihn der Stängel mit einem Dorn.

„Autsch!" schrie er und zog seine Hand zurück. Der Dorn war winzig, kaum wahrnehmbar, aber es tat mehr weh, als es sollte. Grummelton schimpfte und rieb seinen Finger. „Dummer Garten."

Der Riese drehte sich um, um zu gehen, aber etwas hielt ihn auf. Trotz seiner selbst war Grummelton neugierig. Wie hatte dieser winzige Garten in seinem Königreich aus Staub und Stein überlebt? Wer hatte sich um ihn gekümmert? Warum war er hier?

In den nächsten Tagen kam Grummelton immer wieder zu dem kleinen Garten zurück, jedes Mal mit einem neuen Plan, ihn loszuwerden. Zuerst versuchte er, auf die Steine um ihn herum zu stampfen, aber seine Füße waren zu groß, und er stolperte beinahe. Dann versuchte er, die Blumen samt ihren Wurzeln auszureißen, aber sie rutschten ihm durch die Finger wie Sand. Sogar zu viel Wasser wollte er ihnen geben, in der Hoffnung, sie würden ertrinken. Doch stattdessen gedieh der Garten. Die Blumen blühten noch heller, und der kleine Vogel sang lauter als je zuvor.

Frustriert setzte sich Grummelton mit einem Schnauben hin. „Warum willst du nicht verschwinden?“ grummelte er den Garten an. „Was ist so besonders an dir?“

Zu seiner Überraschung antwortete eine winzige Stimme. „Vielleicht liegt es nicht daran, was besonders an dem Garten ist,“ sagte die Stimme. „Sondern was er dir beibringen kann.“

Grummelton schaute verwirrt umher und entdeckte dann einen kleinen, zarten Schmetterling, der auf einer nahegelegenen Narzisse saß. Er schlug träge mit seinen Flügeln und sprach erneut. „Du warst grob und grimmig zu uns, Riese. Gärten brauchen Pflege, Geduld und Freundlichkeit, um zu wachsen.“

„Pflege? Geduld? Bah!“ Grummelton lachte höhnisch. „Ich bin ein Riese! Ich habe keine Zeit für so etwas Dummes.“

„Aber du hast Zeit, Dinge zu zerstören, oder?“ fragte der Schmetterling und flatterte näher an Grummeltons Gesicht. „Warum versuchst du nicht einmal das Gegenteil? Versuch, dem Garten beim Wachsen zu helfen.“

Grummelton wollte gerade widersprechen, hielt aber inne. Er war ein Riese – stark und mächtig – aber all seine Bemühungen, den Garten zu zerstören, waren gescheitert. Was wäre, wenn er etwas anderes versuchte?

Am nächsten Tag kehrte Grummelton zum kleinen Garten zurück, aber diesmal stampfte und grummelte er nicht. Er hockte sich so vorsichtig wie möglich hin und berührte sanft die Blätter. Er versuchte, ihn zu gießen, aber nicht zu viel. Und obwohl es für einen Riesen seiner Größe unbeholfen war, benutzte er seine riesigen Finger, um Unkraut zu jäten.

Zunächst war es schwer. Grummeltons Hände waren groß und unbeholfen, und er zerdrückte versehentlich ein paar Blumen. Er stieß das Nest des kleinen Vogels mehr als einmal um. Aber etwas Unglaubliches geschah: Je vorsichtiger und geduldiger er war, desto mehr wuchs der Garten.

Bald war der kleine Garten nicht mehr so klein. Er breitete sich aus, schlängelte sich durch die Felsen und Ritzen und verwandelte das graue, karge Land in ein Meer von Farben. Blumen aller Art sprossen, Bäume begannen zu wachsen, und Vögel aus nah und fern kamen, um zu singen. Grummeltons Königreich war nicht länger ein Ort der Einöde und des Staubes, sondern einer des Lebens und der Schönheit.

Während der Garten wuchs, wuchs auch Grummeltons Herz. Er stellte fest, dass es ihm leichter und glücklicher machte, sich um etwas so Kleines und Zerbrechliches zu kümmern. Die Kreaturen des Gartens – Bienen, Schmetterlinge und Vögel – wurden seine Freunde, und bald war der einst grimmige Riese am Lächeln. Er begann sogar, eine kleine Melodie zu summen, während er arbeitete.

Eines Tages, als Grummelton den jetzt ausgedehnten Garten bewunderte, landete der kleine Vogel auf seiner Schulter. „Siehst du?" zwitscherte es. „Du brauchtest keine Stärke, um dein Königreich schön zu machen. Nur ein wenig Geduld und Freundlichkeit."

Grummelton lächelte, ein warmes und ehrliches Lächeln. „Ich denke, ich habe tatsächlich etwas gelernt," sagte er leise. „Sogar Riesen haben ein wenig Platz für Magie."

Und von diesem Tag an wurde der Garten das Herz von Grummeltons Königreich. Reisende aus nah und fern kamen, um den wundersamen Garten des einst grimmigen Riesen zu sehen, und Grummelton begrüßte sie alle mit einem Lächeln. Sein Königreich war nicht länger karg, sondern ein Ort, wo das Leben blühte – dank eines kleinen Gartens, viel Geduld und der Freundlichkeit eines Riesen, der lernte, zu lieben.

The Boy Who Could Fly

Everyone thought Tom was just an ordinary boy. He had the same messy brown hair, the same school uniform, and the same baggy trousers as all the other kids at Oakwood Primary School. But Tom had a secret—an extraordinary secret that no one, not even his closest friends, knew.

Tom could fly.

It wasn't like the superheroes in the comic books who soared into the sky with capes billowing behind them. No, Tom's flying was different. It was quieter, gentler. He didn't need a cape or a flashy costume. All he needed was a moment of focus, and off he went, lifting into the air as if gravity had simply forgotten about him.

But for all his remarkable ability, Tom felt like an outsider. While other kids laughed and played, chatting about the latest games or TV shows, Tom found it hard to join in. He was always distracted, afraid that someone might notice the way his feet sometimes hovered just above the ground when he got excited. Or worse—that someone might discover his secret.

So, Tom kept quiet. He hid his talent, only using it when he was completely alone. After school, when the streets were empty and the sky was dark, he would sneak out of his bedroom window and float above the rooftops, watching the world from above. But even then, he felt... different. Like he didn't belong.

One chilly autumn morning, things began to change. Tom was walking to school, hands stuffed deep into his pockets, when he spotted something out of the corner of his eye. A young girl, no older than six, stood on the edge of the road, clutching her teddy bear. She looked up and down the street, but a speeding car was racing towards her.

Tom didn't think. He couldn't.

Before anyone else could react, he leapt into the air. His feet lifted off the ground, and he zoomed over to the girl in a blur. With a soft swoosh, Tom scooped her up just as the car whizzed past. He flew her to the other side of the street, safe and sound.

The little girl blinked in surprise, her eyes wide. "You... you were flying!" she gasped, her tiny voice full of wonder.

Tom's heart raced. He'd been careful for so long, and now this! "It's just between us, okay?" he whispered, setting her down gently.

The girl nodded, her face glowing with excitement, and she ran off, clutching her teddy bear, too thrilled to even ask his name.

As Tom walked the rest of the way to school, he couldn't help but feel a warmth in his chest. He had done something good—something important. But instead of feeling proud, he still felt that familiar sense of being on the outside, looking in.

At school, things were as they always were. Tom sat at the back of the class, watching as his classmates chattered about the weekend's football match. No one talked to him much, except for Pete, a boy with big glasses who was the only one who ever sat with Tom during lunch. Pete was kind and liked science, and he never asked Tom too many questions.

That day during break, Tom overheard a conversation between some kids from the year above. They were standing in a circle, whispering about something.

"Did you hear about Mr. Perkins? His greenhouse collapsed last night in the storm," said one of the boys.

"Yeah, and all his plants are ruined. He'll be so upset—he spends every weekend in that garden," another added.

Tom knew Mr. Perkins, the old man who lived at the corner of his street. He was always kind, and his garden was his pride and joy. Tom's heart sank as he imagined Mr. Perkins discovering the mess.

That night, as the town slept, Tom made a decision. He sneaked out of his bedroom window, the cool breeze ruffling his hair as he floated up into the night sky. He flew over to Mr. Perkins' house, and sure enough, the old man's greenhouse was in ruins. Broken glass scattered across the ground, and plants lay in heaps.

With a deep breath, Tom got to work. He carefully gathered the pieces of glass, flying them over to a recycling bin down the street. Then, using all the strength he could muster, he pushed the fallen beams back into place, one by one. It took hours, but Tom didn't mind. He enjoyed the peaceful quiet of the night as he worked.

By morning, the greenhouse stood tall again. It wasn't perfect—Tom's hands weren't used to such precise work—but it was enough. He planted the flowers back into the soil, making sure they stood straight and proud. Then, just before the sun began to rise, he flew back to his house, slipping into bed with a contented sigh.

The next day at school, Tom overheard more whispers.

"Did you hear about Mr. Perkins' greenhouse? Someone fixed it last night! It's like magic!" one of the kids exclaimed.

Tom smiled to himself, but said nothing. It felt good, knowing he had helped.

Over the next few weeks, Tom's secret life continued. He fixed broken toys that kids had lost in the park, retrieved a balloon that had floated too high for a little boy to reach, and once even helped an old lady who had lost her cat. Every time, he made sure no one saw him, no one knew it was him. And with each good deed, Tom felt a little less like an outsider.

One afternoon, as Tom sat on the swings at the edge of the playground, Pete wandered over and plopped down beside him. "You know, there's been a lot of strange things happening around here," Pete said, adjusting his glasses. "Good things. Like someone's been watching over everyone, helping out. It's weird, but kind of nice."

Tom glanced sideways at Pete, wondering if he suspected anything. But Pete just smiled and pushed his glasses further up his nose. "I bet it's someone who doesn't care about getting attention. Someone who just wants to do the right thing."

Tom's heart swelled. For the first time, he felt like someone understood him, even if Pete didn't know the whole truth.

From that day on, Tom didn't feel like an outsider anymore. Sure, no one knew about his flying, but that didn't matter. He had found his place, not by standing out or showing off, but by helping others in his own quiet, extraordinary way.

And as long as there were people who needed a little help—whether they knew it or not—Tom, the boy who could fly, would be there.

Der Junge, der fliegen konnte

Alle dachten, Tom sei nur ein gewöhnlicher Junge. Er hatte dasselbe zerzauste braune Haar, dieselbe Schuluniform und dieselben weiten Hosen wie all die anderen Kinder der Oakwood Grundschule. Aber Tom hatte ein Geheimnis—ein außergewöhnliches Geheimnis, das niemand kannte, nicht einmal seine engsten Freunde.

Tom konnte fliegen.

Es war nicht wie bei den Superhelden in den Comics, die mit wehenden Capes in den Himmel schossen. Nein, Toms Fliegen war anders. Es war leiser, sanfter. Er brauchte keinen Umhang und kein auffälliges Kostüm. Alles, was er brauchte, war ein Moment der Konzentration, und schon hob er ab, als ob die Schwerkraft ihn einfach vergessen hätte.

Doch trotz seiner bemerkenswerten Fähigkeit fühlte sich Tom wie ein Außenseiter. Während die anderen Kinder lachten und spielten und über die neuesten Spiele oder Fernsehsendungen plauderten, fiel es Tom schwer, sich einzubringen. Er war immer abgelenkt, aus Angst, dass jemand bemerkte, wie seine Füße manchmal gerade über dem Boden schwebten, wenn er aufgeregt war. Oder schlimmer noch—dass jemand sein Geheimnis entdeckte.

Also blieb Tom still. Er versteckte sein Talent und nutzte es nur, wenn er ganz allein war. Nach der Schule, wenn die Straßen leer und der Himmel dunkel war, schlüpfte er aus seinem Schlafzimmerfenster und schwebte über die Dächer, beobachtete die Welt von oben. Doch selbst dann fühlte er sich... anders. Als gehörte er nicht dazu.

Eines kühlen Herbstmorgens begann sich alles zu verändern. Tom ging zur Schule, die Hände tief in den Taschen vergraben, als er aus dem Augenwinkel etwas bemerkte. Ein kleines Mädchen, nicht älter als sechs, stand am Straßenrand und hielt ihren Teddybär fest umschlungen. Sie schaute die Straße auf und ab, doch ein rasendes Auto raste auf sie zu.

Tom dachte nicht nach. Er konnte es nicht.

Bevor jemand anders reagieren konnte, sprang er in die Luft. Seine Füße hoben sich vom Boden, und er sauste wie ein Blitz zu dem Mädchen. Mit einem sanften Schwung nahm Tom sie auf, genau als das Auto vorbeirauschte. Er flog sie auf die andere Straßenseite, sicher und geborgen.

Das kleine Mädchen blinzelte überrascht, ihre Augen weit aufgerissen. „Du... du bist geflogen!", stammelte sie, ihre kleine Stimme voller Staunen.

Toms Herz raste. Er war so lange vorsichtig gewesen, und jetzt das! „Es bleibt nur zwischen uns, okay?", flüsterte er und setzte sie sanft ab.

Das Mädchen nickte, ihr Gesicht strahlte vor Aufregung, und sie rannte davon, ihren Teddybär fest umklammert, zu aufgeregt, um nach seinem Namen zu fragen.

Als Tom den restlichen Weg zur Schule ging, konnte er nicht anders, als ein warmes Gefühl in seiner Brust zu spüren. Er hatte etwas Gutes getan—etwas Wichtiges. Doch anstatt stolz zu sein, fühlte er immer noch dieses vertraute Gefühl, außen vor zu sein.

In der Schule war alles wie immer. Tom saß hinten in der Klasse und sah zu, wie seine Mitschüler über das Fußballspiel am Wochenende plauderten. Niemand sprach viel mit ihm, außer Pete, einem Jungen mit großen Brillen, der der Einzige war, der während des Mittagessens jemals mit Tom saß. Pete war nett und mochte Wissenschaft, und er stellte Tom nie zu viele Fragen.

An diesem Tag während der Pause hörte Tom ein Gespräch zwischen einigen Kindern aus der höheren Jahrgangsstufe. Sie standen im Kreis und flüsterten über etwas.

„Hast du von Mr. Perkins gehört? Sein Gewächshaus ist letzte Nacht im Sturm eingestürzt", sagte einer der Jungen.

„Ja, und all seine Pflanzen sind ruiniert. Er wird so traurig sein—er verbringt jedes Wochenende in diesem Garten", fügte ein anderer hinzu.

Tom kannte Mr. Perkins, den alten Mann, der an der Ecke seiner Straße wohnte. Er war immer freundlich, und sein Garten war sein Stolz und seine Freude. Toms Herz sank, als er sich vorstellte, wie Mr. Perkins das Chaos entdeckte.

In dieser Nacht, als die Stadt schlief, traf Tom eine Entscheidung. Er schlüpfte aus seinem Schlafzimmerfenster, der kühle Wind zerzauste sein Haar, als er in den Nachthimmel schwebte. Er flog zu Mr. Perkins' Haus, und tatsächlich war das Gewächshaus des alten Mannes in Trümmern. Zerbrochenes Glas lag überall auf dem Boden, und Pflanzen lagen in Haufen.

Mit einem tiefen Atemzug machte Tom sich an die Arbeit. Er sammelte vorsichtig die Glasscherben und flog sie zu einem Recyclingbehälter die Straße hinunter. Dann, mit all der Kraft, die er aufbringen konnte, schob er die umgefallenen Balken eins nach dem anderen wieder an ihren Platz. Es dauerte Stunden, aber das machte Tom nichts aus. Er genoss die friedliche Stille der Nacht, während er arbeitete.

Am Morgen stand das Gewächshaus wieder hoch und stolz. Es war nicht perfekt—Toms Hände waren nicht an so präzise Arbeiten gewöhnt—aber es war genug. Er pflanzte die Blumen zurück in die Erde und sorgte dafür, dass sie aufrecht und stolz standen. Dann, kurz bevor die Sonne aufging, flog er zurück zu seinem Haus und schlüpfte mit einem zufriedenen Seufzer ins Bett.

Am nächsten Tag in der Schule hörte Tom wieder Gemurmel.

„Hast du von Mr. Perkins' Gewächshaus gehört? Jemand hat es letzte Nacht repariert! Es ist wie Magie!", rief eines der Kinder.

Tom lächelte in sich hinein, sagte aber nichts. Es fühlte sich gut an, zu wissen, dass er geholfen hatte.

In den nächsten Wochen ging Toms geheimes Leben weiter. Er reparierte kaputte Spielzeuge, die Kinder im Park verloren hatten, holte einen Ballon zurück, der zu hoch für einen kleinen Jungen geflogen war, und half einmal sogar einer alten Dame, die ihre Katze verloren hatte. Jedes Mal sorgte er dafür, dass ihn niemand sah, dass niemand wusste, dass er es war. Und mit jeder guten Tat fühlte Tom sich ein bisschen weniger wie ein Außenseiter.

Einen Nachmittag, als Tom auf der Schaukel am Rand des Spielplatzes saß, kam Pete vorbei und plumpste neben ihm nieder. „Weißt du, hier passieren viele seltsame Dinge", sagte Pete und schob sich die Brille zurecht. „Gute Dinge. Es ist, als ob jemand über alle wacht und hilft. Es ist komisch, aber irgendwie nett."

Tom sah Pete seitlich an und fragte sich, ob er etwas ahnte. Aber Pete lächelte nur und schob seine Brille weiter auf die Nase. „Ich wette, es ist jemand, der sich nicht um Aufmerksamkeit kümmert. Jemand, der einfach das Richtige tun will."

Toms Herz schwoll an. Zum ersten Mal fühlte er sich, als ob ihn jemand verstand, auch wenn Pete nicht die ganze Wahrheit kannte.

Von diesem Tag an fühlte sich Tom nicht mehr wie ein Außenseiter. Sicher, niemand wusste von seinem Fliegen, aber das spielte keine Rolle. Er hatte seinen Platz gefunden, nicht indem er herausstach oder angeben wollte, sondern indem er anderen auf seine eigene stille, außergewöhnliche Weise half.

Und solange es Menschen gab, die ein wenig Hilfe benötigten—ob sie es wussten oder nicht—würde Tom, der Junge, der fliegen konnte, da sein.

The Curious Case of the Talking Teapot

In the quiet, sleepy village of Willowbrook, nothing much ever happened. It was the kind of place where people knew each other's business, where life was predictable and safe. Children played the same games in the same parks, and the adults gossiped over tea in the same little cafes. But one ordinary Tuesday afternoon, something extraordinary happened to a girl named Emily.

Emily was an adventurous child, though she lived in a village where adventure was rare. With wild, curly hair and a curious mind, she loved wandering around Willowbrook's winding streets, always hoping to stumble upon something exciting. That afternoon, while poking around in the village's antique shop, Emily's life was about to change.

The shop was a musty, cluttered place filled with old clocks, dusty furniture, and piles of forgotten trinkets. It was Emily's favorite spot, where she could let her imagination run wild. She imagined the clocks were enchanted, the mirrors showed secret worlds, and the ancient books were full of untold mysteries.

As she meandered through the aisles, something on a high shelf caught her eye—a small, delicate teapot, painted with faded golden flowers. It was chipped in a few places, and the once-shiny surface was now dull. But something about it seemed special, almost magical.

Curiosity getting the better of her, Emily reached up and pulled the teapot down from the shelf. The moment her fingers touched the porcelain, a strange thing happened.

"Ah, finally! About time someone noticed me!" a voice said, making Emily jump.

She looked around, startled. The shop was empty, except for Mrs. Crawley, the shopkeeper, who was busy reading a magazine behind the counter.

"Down here, child!" the voice said again, this time more impatient.

Emily's eyes widened. The voice was coming from... the teapot!

"You... you can talk?" Emily stammered, staring at the teapot in disbelief.

"Well, obviously!" huffed the teapot, as if it was the most normal thing in the world. "I've been sitting on that shelf for decades, waiting for someone with a bit of imagination to find me."

Emily blinked, trying to make sense of what was happening. "Who are you?"

"I'm not just any old teapot," the teapot said proudly. "I've had many owners, each with their own stories—some extraordinary, some downright ridiculous. Oh, the tales I could tell you, child! Pirates, wizards, kings—you name it!"

Emily's heart skipped a beat. A talking teapot that knew stories of pirates and wizards? This was the adventure she had been waiting for!

"Tell me more!" she said, her eyes shining with excitement. "Who were your owners? What did they do?"

The teapot let out a satisfied little sigh. "Ah, let me start with Captain Horatio Blackbeard—no relation to the infamous pirate, but just as fierce. He sailed the high seas in search of treasure, and I was his prized possession, you see. Not because I was valuable—oh no—but because I held the map to the greatest treasure of all."

Emily leaned in closer, utterly captivated. "A treasure map?"

"Indeed," the teapot said, its voice dropping to a conspiratorial whisper. "Inside my spout, hidden in secret ink, was the map to Skull Island. Oh, the adventures we had! Captain Blackbeard fought off sea monsters and rival pirates, all while making sure to have a cup of tea, of course."

Emily giggled. The idea of a fearsome pirate captain sipping tea was too funny.

"But alas," the teapot continued, "the map was lost when a particularly large wave washed over the deck. Captain Blackbeard was heartbroken. He tossed me aside, thinking I was just a useless old teapot after that."

Emily frowned. "That's so unfair! You're amazing!"

"Oh, I know, dear, I know," the teapot said smugly. "But that's not even the best part. After Blackbeard, I ended up in the hands of a wizard—a rather forgetful one named Alazar. Now, he wasn't your typical wizard, mind you. He was always misplacing his spell books, losing his wand, or turning himself into a toad by accident."

Emily giggled again. "What did you do for him?"

"Well, I kept his tea warm, of course," the teapot said, as if this was the most important job in the world. "But I also helped him remember his spells. Every time he was in the middle of a particularly tricky one and forgot the words, I'd whisper them to him. That's how he managed to conjure up a rainbow over the village of Frostwind—by listening to a teapot!"

Emily clapped her hands in delight. "A wizard and a rainbow! That's incredible!"

The teapot gave a little sniff. "Oh, it was nothing, really. Alazar was grateful, but like all wizards, he was rather absent-minded. Eventually, he misplaced me during a spell gone wrong, and I ended up in a royal palace—owned by none other than King Leopold the Third."

"A king?!" Emily's eyes were wide with awe.

"Indeed," the teapot said grandly. "King Leopold was a kind ruler, but terribly indecisive. He couldn't make a decision without consulting every single advisor in the land, including me! 'Should I wear the red robes or the blue robes?' he'd ask me.

'Should I tax the farmers less or more this year?' And I'd tell him, 'Leopold, dear, go with your gut!'"

"Did he listen to you?"

"Well, he certainly tried," the teapot chuckled. "But kings don't always follow advice, even from magical teapots. Still, it was a splendid life—until one day, during a royal banquet, I was accidentally knocked off the table by a clumsy servant and ended up in a box of old relics. And, well, here I am, in this little shop."

Emily looked at the teapot with wonder. How could something so special have ended up forgotten on a dusty shelf?

"You've had such an amazing life," she said softly. "And so many adventures."

The teapot seemed to smile, if teapots could smile. "Yes, indeed. But you know, child, there's one thing I've learned through all these years. The greatest magic of all is not in the treasures or the spells or the royal palaces. It's in the stories we tell. Stories make the world bigger, more colorful, more exciting."

Emily nodded. She had always loved stories, but hearing it from a talking teapot made it feel even more special.

The teapot's voice softened. "And now, my dear, it's time for you to create your own stories. You've got a curious heart and a bright mind. Who knows what adventures you'll have?"

Emily smiled, her heart filled with warmth. She felt as if she had discovered a secret part of the world that no one else knew existed. And in that moment, she knew the teapot was right—stories were magic. And she was going to make sure hers were just as extraordinary.

With one last look at the talking teapot, Emily carefully placed it back on the shelf.

"Thank you," she whispered.

And as she left the shop, she could have sworn she heard the teapot's voice, faint but clear.

"Go on, child. Make your story."

Der seltsame Fall der sprechenden Teekanne

Im ruhigen, schläfrigen Dorf Willowbrook passierte nie viel. Es war die Art von Ort, wo die Leute die Angelegenheiten der anderen kannten, wo das Leben vorhersehbar und sicher war. Die Kinder spielten die gleichen Spiele in denselben Parks, und die Erwachsenen plauderten bei einer Tasse Tee in denselben kleinen Cafés. Doch an einem gewöhnlichen Dienstagnachmittag geschah etwas Außergewöhnliches mit einem Mädchen namens Emily.

Emily war ein abenteuerlustiges Kind, obwohl sie in einem Dorf lebte, in dem Abenteuer selten waren. Mit wildem, lockigem Haar und einem neugierigen Geist liebte sie es, durch die gewundenen Straßen von Willowbrook zu wandern, immer in der Hoffnung, auf etwas Aufregendes zu stoßen. An diesem Nachmittag, während sie im Antiquitätenladen des Dorfes stöberte, sollte sich Emilys Leben verändern.

Der Laden war ein muffiger, überladener Ort, gefüllt mit alten Uhren, staubigen Möbeln und Haufen vergessener Trödel. Es war Emilys Lieblingsplatz, an dem sie ihrer Fantasie freien Lauf lassen konnte. Sie stellte sich vor, die Uhren seien verzaubert, die Spiegel zeigten geheime Welten, und die alten Bücher seien voller unentdeckter Geheimnisse.

Als sie durch die Gänge schlenderte, fiel ihr etwas auf einem hohen Regal ins Auge – eine kleine, zarte Teekanne, bemalt mit verblassten goldenen Blumen. Sie war an einigen Stellen abgebrochen, und die einst glänzende Oberfläche war jetzt stumpf. Aber etwas an ihr schien besonders, fast magisch.

Die Neugier überkam sie, und Emily griff nach der Teekanne und zog sie vom Regal herunter. In dem Moment, in dem ihre Finger das Porzellan berührten, geschah etwas Seltsames.

„Ah, endlich! Höchste Zeit, dass mich jemand bemerkt!" sagte eine Stimme, die Emily erschrecken ließ.

Sie schaute sich startled um. Der Laden war leer, abgesehen von Mrs. Crawley, der Ladenbesitzerin, die hinter dem Tresen eine Zeitschrift las.

„Hier unten, Kind!" sagte die Stimme erneut, diesmal ungeduldig.

Emilys Augen weiteten sich. Die Stimme kam von... der Teekanne!

„Du... du kannst sprechen?" stammelte Emily und starrte die Teekanne ungläubig an.

„Natürlich!" schnaufte die Teekanne, als wäre es das Normalste auf der Welt. „Ich habe jahrzehntelang auf diesem Regal gesessen und gewartet, dass mich jemand mit ein wenig Fantasie findet."

Emily blinzelte, versuchte zu begreifen, was geschah. „Wer bist du?"

„Ich bin nicht einfach irgendeine alte Teekanne," sagte die Teekanne stolz. „Ich hatte viele Besitzer, jeder mit eigenen

Geschichten – einige außergewöhnlich, andere völlig lächerlich. Oh, die Geschichten, die ich dir erzählen könnte, Kind! Piraten, Zauberer, Könige – nenn es einfach!"

Emilys Herz machte einen Sprung. Eine sprechende Teekanne, die Geschichten von Piraten und Zauberern kannte? Das war das Abenteuer, auf das sie gewartet hatte!

„Erzähl mir mehr!" sagte sie, ihre Augen funkelten vor Aufregung. „Wer waren deine Besitzer? Was haben sie gemacht?"

Die Teekanne gab ein zufriedenes Seufzen von sich. „Ah, lass mich mit Kapitän Horatio Blackbeard anfangen – keine Verwandtschaft zum berüchtigten Piraten, aber genauso wild. Er segelte über die hohen See auf der Suche nach Schätzen, und ich war sein wertvollster Besitz, verstehst du? Nicht, weil ich wertvoll war – oh nein – sondern weil ich die Karte zum größten Schatz von allen hielt."

Emily beugte sich näher, völlig fasziniert. „Eine Schatzkarte?"

„In der Tat," sagte die Teekanne und senkte ihre Stimme zu einem verschwörerischen Flüstern. „In meinem Ausguss, verborgen in geheimen Tinte, war die Karte zu Skull Island. Oh, die Abenteuer, die wir hatten! Kapitän Blackbeard kämpfte gegen Seeungeheuer und rivalisierende Piraten, während er natürlich dafür sorgte, eine Tasse Tee zu genießen."

Emily kicherte. Die Vorstellung eines furchtlosen Piratenkapitäns, der Tee trinkt, war zu lustig.

„Aber alas," fuhr die Teekanne fort, „ging die Karte verloren, als eine besonders große Welle über das Deck schwappte. Kapitän

Blackbeard war untröstlich. Er warf mich beiseite, weil er dachte, ich sei nur eine nutzlose alte Teekanne danach."

Emily runzelte die Stirn. „Das ist so unfair! Du bist erstaunlich!"

„Oh, das weiß ich, mein Kind, das weiß ich," sagte die Teekanne selbstgefällig. „Aber das ist noch nicht einmal der beste Teil. Nach Blackbeard landete ich in den Händen eines Zauberers – eines recht vergesslichen namens Alazar. Nun, er war nicht dein typischer Zauberer, versteht sich. Er verlor ständig seine Zauberbücher, seine Zauberstäbe oder verwandelte sich versehentlich in einen Frosch."

Emily kicherte wieder. „Was hast du für ihn getan?"

„Nun, ich hielt seinen Tee warm, natürlich," sagte die Teekanne, als wäre dies der wichtigste Job der Welt. „Aber ich half ihm auch, sich an seine Zauber zu erinnern. Jedes Mal, wenn er gerade inmitten eines besonders kniffligen Zaubers war und die Worte vergaß, flüsterte ich sie ihm zu. So schaffte er es, einen Regenbogen über dem Dorf Frostwind heraufzubeschwören – indem er auf eine Teekanne hörte!"

Emily klatschte begeistert in die Hände. „Ein Zauberer und ein Regenbogen! Das ist unglaublich!"

Die Teekanne schniefte ein wenig. „Oh, das war nichts, wirklich. Alazar war dankbar, aber wie alle Zauberer war er ziemlich zerstreut. Schließlich verlor er mich während eines missratene Zaubers, und ich landete in einem königlichen Palast – im Besitz von niemand anderem als König Leopold dem Dritten."

„Ein König?!" Emilys Augen waren weit vor Ehrfurcht.

„In der Tat," sagte die Teekanne großartig. „König Leopold war ein gütiger Herrscher, aber furchtbar unentschlossen. Er konnte keine Entscheidung treffen, ohne jeden einzelnen Berater im Land zu konsultieren, einschließlich mir! ‚Soll ich die roten Roben oder die blauen Roben tragen?' fragte er mich. ‚Soll ich die Bauern dieses Jahr weniger oder mehr besteuern?' Und ich sagte ihm: ‚Leopold, mein Lieber, hör auf dein Bauchgefühl!'"

„Hat er auf dich gehört?"

„Nun, er hat es jedenfalls versucht," lachte die Teekanne. „Aber Könige folgen nicht immer dem Rat, selbst von magischen Teekannen. Trotzdem war es ein prächtiges Leben – bis eines Tages, während eines königlichen Banketts, ich versehentlich von einem tollpatschigen Diener vom Tisch gestoßen wurde und in einer Kiste mit alten Relikten landete. Und nun bin ich hier, in diesem kleinen Laden."

Emily schaute die Teekanne mit Staunen an. Wie konnte etwas so Besonderes auf einem staubigen Regal vergessen worden sein?

„Du hast ein so erstaunliches Leben gehabt," sagte sie leise. „Und so viele Abenteuer."

Die Teekanne schien zu lächeln, wenn Teekannen lächeln könnten. „Ja, in der Tat. Aber weißt du, Kind, eines habe ich durch all diese Jahre gelernt. Die größte Magie von allen liegt nicht in den Schätzen oder den Zaubern oder den königlichen Palästen. Sie liegt in den Geschichten, die wir erzählen. Geschichten machen die Welt größer, bunter, aufregender."

Emily nickte. Sie hatte Geschichten schon immer geliebt, aber es von einer sprechenden Teekanne zu hören, machte es noch spezieller.

Die Stimme der Teekanne wurde sanfter. „Und jetzt, mein Liebling, ist es Zeit für dich, deine eigenen Geschichten zu schaffen. Du hast ein neugieriges Herz und einen hellen Geist. Wer weiß, welche Abenteuer du erleben wirst?"

Emily lächelte, ihr Herz war erfüllt von Wärme. Sie hatte das Gefühl, als hätte sie einen geheimen Teil der Welt entdeckt, den sonst niemand kannte. Und in diesem Moment wusste sie, dass die Teekanne recht hatte – Geschichten waren Magie. Und sie wurde dafür sorgen, dass ihre genauso außergewöhnlich waren.

Mit einem letzten Blick auf die sprechende Teekanne stellte Emily sie vorsichtig wieder ins Regal.

„Danke," flüsterte sie.

Und als sie den Laden verließ, konnte sie schwören, dass sie die Stimme der Teekanne hörte, leise, aber klar.

„Mach weiter, Kind. Erschaffe deine Geschichte."

The Elephant Who Lost His Shadow

There was once a gentle elephant named Ellington who lived in a lush and peaceful forest. Ellington was known for his calm nature and kind heart, always helping the smaller animals, guiding lost travelers, and offering his broad back as a comfortable seat for any creature in need. But despite all this, Ellington had one small insecurity—his shadow.

You see, Ellington's shadow was enormous, even larger than he was, and it followed him everywhere. When the other animals noticed his giant shadow stretching out across the fields, they would giggle, and some would even hide behind it during games. Ellington didn't mind too much, but deep down, he felt his shadow was just a bit too big. It made him feel clumsy, like he was taking up too much space in the world.

One bright morning, as the sun rose and cast its golden rays through the trees, Ellington lumbered to his favorite spot by the river to have a drink. But as he bent down to sip the cool water, something strange caught his eye. The reflection in the water showed his big, gray body... but there was no shadow beside it.

Ellington blinked. He looked behind him, at the ground, and then around at the trees. His shadow was gone.

"Where is it?" he murmured, confused. He stomped his large foot to make sure it wasn't just playing a trick on him, but no shadow appeared. Ellington searched all around the clearing, under trees, behind bushes, and even in the river, but his shadow was nowhere to be found.

Panic slowly crept into his heart. His shadow had always been there, like a constant companion, even if it sometimes embarrassed him. Now, without it, he felt strangely incomplete.

"I must find it," he thought. "I can't be an elephant without my shadow."

So, Ellington set off on a journey across the forest, determined to find his missing shadow. As he walked, the sun climbed higher, but still no shadow appeared beneath his large feet.

Along the way, Ellington met a cheerful squirrel named Saffron, who was busy gathering acorns.

"Hello, Ellington!" Saffron called. "What's wrong? You look worried."

"I've lost my shadow," Ellington said sadly. "I've looked everywhere, but I can't find it."

Saffron tilted her head and looked at the ground around Ellington's feet. "That's odd. Shadows don't usually just disappear. Have you tried asking the wind? It carries things far and wide—it might know where your shadow went."

"That's a good idea," Ellington said, hopeful.

He lifted his trunk high into the air and called out to the wind, "Oh wind, have you seen my shadow? Where has it gone?"

The wind rustled through the leaves and sighed softly as it whispered in his ear, "Your shadow is on a journey of its own, Ellington. It has wandered off to find its purpose, just as you are now doing."

Ellington's heart sank. His shadow was on its own adventure without him? "But I need it to be whole," he said.

The wind whispered again, "Perhaps being whole isn't about what you think you've lost, but what you discover along the way."

Ellington didn't quite understand, but he thanked the wind and continued his journey.

Next, he came across a wise old tortoise named Tilda, who was slowly making her way across the forest floor.

"Hello, Tilda," Ellington greeted her. "I've lost my shadow, and I don't know how to be myself without it."

Tilda paused, looking up at the large elephant. "Do you feel any different without it?" she asked in her slow, steady voice.

"I... I feel strange," Ellington admitted. "I've always had my shadow, even though it was so big and made me feel awkward. Without it, I don't feel like myself."

Tilda nodded. "Sometimes, the things we think we need to be whole are not as important as we believe. Have you ever considered that maybe, just maybe, your shadow is not what defines you?"

Ellington frowned. "But if I'm not my shadow, then what am I?"

"You are you, Ellington," Tilda said with a smile. "Whether your shadow is with you or not, you are still the same gentle, kind elephant who helps everyone in the forest."

Ellington hadn't thought of it that way before. Maybe Tilda was right. Maybe his shadow didn't make him who he was. But even so, he missed it.

He thanked Tilda and continued on his journey, climbing hills and crossing rivers in search of his shadow. Days passed, and as Ellington wandered through meadows and valleys, he began to realize something. Without his shadow, he moved more freely. He no longer worried about where it stretched or how much space it took up. He could walk, dance, and even spin in circles without feeling like he was tripping over himself.

He began to feel lighter, not because he had lost his shadow, but because he had stopped worrying about it. He started enjoying the simple pleasures of his journey—the rustle of leaves underfoot, the scent of wildflowers, and the company of the animals he met along the way. He helped a family of ducks cross a river, played hide-and-seek with some mischievous rabbits, and even learned a new song from a group of birds.

One evening, as the sun was setting and casting long shadows over the land, Ellington found himself on a hill overlooking the forest. The sky was painted with hues of pink and gold, and the world felt calm and still.

Suddenly, something flickered at his feet. Ellington looked down, and there, stretching out beside him, was his shadow. It had returned.

Ellington smiled, but this time, it wasn't a smile of relief. He no longer felt incomplete without his shadow. Instead, he felt whole—because he had learned that being whole wasn't about having all the parts we think we need. It was about embracing who we are, flaws and all.

His shadow, which had once seemed so large and cumbersome, was now just a part of him—not something to be ashamed of, but something to accept.

As the stars began to twinkle above, Ellington settled down on the hill, his shadow curling beside him like an old friend. He closed his eyes, feeling peaceful and content, knowing that he was enough just as he was.

And from that day on, whether his shadow was with him or not, Ellington knew that being whole didn't mean being perfect. It meant being kind, patient, and true to himself—just as he had always been.

Der Elefant, der seinen Schatten verlor

Es war einmal ein sanfter Elefant namens Ellington, der in einem üppigen und friedlichen Wald lebte. Ellington war bekannt für seine ruhige Art und sein gutes Herz. Er half stets den kleineren Tieren, führte verlorene Wanderer und bot seinen breiten Rücken als bequemen Platz für jedes bedürftige Wesen an. Doch trotz all dem hatte Ellington eine kleine Unsicherheit – seinen Schatten.

Siehst du, Ellingtons Schatten war riesig, sogar größer als er selbst, und er folgte ihm überallhin. Wenn die anderen Tiere seinen riesigen Schatten über die Wiesen gleiten sahen, kicherten sie, und manche versteckten sich sogar während der Spiele hinter ihm. Ellington machte sich nicht allzu viele Gedanken darüber, aber tief im Inneren fühlte er, dass sein Schatten ein wenig zu groß war. Er ließ ihn ungeschickt erscheinen, als würde er zu viel Platz in der Welt einnehmen.

An einem hellen Morgen, als die Sonne aufging und ihre goldenen Strahlen durch die Bäume warf, trottete Ellington zu seinem Lieblingsplatz am Fluss, um einen Schluck Wasser zu trinken. Doch als er sich bückte, um das kühle Wasser zu nippen, fiel ihm etwas Merkwürdiges auf. Die Spiegelung im Wasser zeigte seinen großen, grauen Körper... aber es war kein Schatten neben ihm.

Ellington blinzelte. Er schaute hinter sich, auf den Boden, und dann um die Bäume herum. Sein Schatten war verschwunden.

„Wo ist er?", murmelte er verwirrt. Er stampfte mit seinem großen Fuß, um sicherzugehen, dass ihm nicht nur ein Streich gespielt wurde, aber kein Schatten erschien. Ellington suchte überall in der Lichtung, unter den Bäumen, hinter den Büschen und sogar im Fluss, aber sein Schatten war nirgends zu finden.

Panik schlich sich langsam in sein Herz. Sein Schatten war immer da gewesen, wie ein ständiger Begleiter, auch wenn er ihn manchmal beschämte. Jetzt, ohne ihn, fühlte er sich seltsam unvollständig.

„Ich muss ihn finden", dachte er. „Ich kann kein Elefant ohne meinen Schatten sein."

So machte sich Ellington auf eine Reise durch den Wald, entschlossen, seinen verschwundenen Schatten zu finden. Während er ging, stieg die Sonne höher, aber immer noch erschien kein Schatten unter seinen großen Füßen.

Auf dem Weg traf Ellington ein fröhliches Eichhörnchen namens Saffron, das damit beschäftigt war, Eicheln zu sammeln.

„Hallo, Ellington!", rief Saffron. „Was ist los? Du siehst besorgt aus."

„Ich habe meinen Schatten verloren", sagte Ellington traurig. „Ich habe überall gesucht, aber ich kann ihn nicht finden."

Saffron neigte den Kopf und schaute auf den Boden rund um Ellingtons Füße. „Das ist seltsam. Schatten verschwinden normalerweise nicht einfach. Hast du schon versucht, den Wind zu fragen? Er trägt Dinge weit und breit – vielleicht weiß er, wo dein Schatten geblieben ist."

„Das ist eine gute Idee", sagte Ellington hoffnungsvoll.

Er hob seinen Rüssel hoch in die Luft und rief dem Wind zu: „Oh Wind, hast du meinen Schatten gesehen? Wo ist er hin?"

Der Wind rauschte durch die Blätter und seufzte sanft, während er ihm ins Ohr flüsterte: „Dein Schatten ist auf einer eigenen Reise, Ellington. Er ist fortgegangen, um seinen Zweck zu finden, so wie du es jetzt tust."

Ellingtons Herz sank. Sein Schatten war auf seinem eigenen Abenteuer ohne ihn? „Aber ich brauche ihn, um ganz zu sein", sagte er.

Der Wind flüsterte erneut: „Vielleicht geht es beim Ganzsein nicht darum, was du glaubst, verloren zu haben, sondern darum, was du auf dem Weg entdeckst."

Ellington verstand nicht ganz, aber er dankte dem Wind und setzte seine Reise fort.

Als Nächstes traf er auf eine weise alte Schildkröte namens Tilda, die sich langsam über den Waldboden bewegte.

„Hallo, Tilda", begrüßte Ellington sie. „Ich habe meinen Schatten verloren, und ich weiß nicht, wie ich ohne ihn ich selbst sein kann."

Tilda hielt inne und schaute zu dem großen Elefanten auf. „Fühlst du dich ohne ihn anders?", fragte sie in ihrer langsamen, ruhigen Stimme.

„Ich... ich fühle mich seltsam", gab Ellington zu. „Ich hatte immer meinen Schatten, auch wenn er so groß war und mich ungeschickt fühlte. Ohne ihn fühle ich mich nicht wie ich selbst."

Tilda nickte. „Manchmal sind die Dinge, von denen wir denken, dass wir sie brauchen, um ganz zu sein, nicht so wichtig, wie wir glauben. Hast du jemals darüber nachgedacht, dass vielleicht, nur vielleicht, dein Schatten nicht das ist, was dich definiert?"

Ellington runzelte die Stirn. „Aber wenn ich nicht mein Schatten bin, was bin ich dann?"

„Du bist du, Ellington", sagte Tilda mit einem Lächeln. „Ob dein Schatten bei dir ist oder nicht, du bist immer noch derselbe sanfte, freundliche Elefant, der allen im Wald hilft."

Ellington hatte noch nie so darüber nachgedacht. Vielleicht hatte Tilda recht. Vielleicht machte ihn sein Schatten nicht zu dem, was er war. Aber trotzdem vermisste er ihn.

Er dankte Tilda und setzte seine Reise fort, erklomm Hügel und überquerte Flüsse auf der Suche nach seinem Schatten. Tage vergingen, und während Ellington durch Wiesen und Täler wanderte, begann er etwas zu erkennen. Ohne seinen Schatten bewegte er sich freier. Er machte sich keine Gedanken mehr darüber, wo er sich erstreckte oder wie viel Platz er einnahm.

Er konnte gehen, tanzen und sogar im Kreis drehen, ohne das Gefühl zu haben, über sich selbst zu stolpern.

Er begann sich leichter zu fühlen, nicht weil er seinen Schatten verloren hatte, sondern weil er aufgehört hatte, sich darüber Sorgen zu machen. Er begann die einfachen Freuden seiner Reise zu genießen – das Rascheln der Blätter unter seinen Füßen, den Duft der Wildblumen und die Gesellschaft der Tiere, die er auf dem Weg traf. Er half einer Entenfamilie, einen Fluss zu überqueren, spielte Verstecken mit einigen schelmischen Kaninchen und lernte sogar ein neues Lied von einer Gruppe von Vögeln.

Eines Abends, als die Sonne unterging und lange Schatten über das Land warf, fand sich Ellington auf einem Hügel wieder, der den Wald überblickte. Der Himmel war in Rosa- und Goldtönen gemalt, und die Welt fühlte sich ruhig und still an.

Plötzlich flackerte etwas zu seinen Füßen. Ellington schaute nach unten, und dort, neben ihm, erstreckte sich sein Schatten. Er war zurückgekehrt.

Ellington lächelte, aber dieses Mal war es kein Lächeln der Erleichterung. Er fühlte sich nicht mehr unvollständig ohne seinen Schatten. Stattdessen fühlte er sich ganz – denn er hatte gelernt, dass Ganzsein nicht darum geht, alle Teile zu haben, die wir glauben zu brauchen. Es geht darum, zu akzeptieren, wer wir sind, mit all unseren Fehlern.

Sein Schatten, der einst so groß und sperrig schien, war jetzt nur ein Teil von ihm – nichts, wofür man sich schämen müsste, sondern etwas, das man akzeptieren konnte.

Als die Sterne zu funkeln begannen, ließ sich Ellington auf dem Hügel nieder, sein Schatten schlang sich neben ihn wie ein alter Freund. Er schloss die Augen, fühlte sich friedlich und zufrieden und wusste, dass er genau so genug war, wie er war.

Und von diesem Tag an, ob sein Schatten bei ihm war oder nicht, wusste Ellington, dass Ganzsein nicht bedeutete, perfekt zu sein. Es bedeutete, freundlich, geduldig und treu zu sich selbst zu sein – genau so, wie er es immer gewesen war.

The Great Balloon Adventure

It was an ordinary Friday afternoon in the small town of Bumblebrook when something extraordinary happened. Four kids—Max, Lily, Finn, and Ruby—were sitting in class, bored out of their minds, when their teacher, Mrs. Crumble, burst through the door waving a golden envelope.

"Children!" she exclaimed, her face glowing with excitement. "You won't believe what has just arrived!"

Max raised an eyebrow. Lily sat up straighter, intrigued. Finn, who was always daydreaming, blinked himself back to reality. And Ruby, well, Ruby was already imagining something grand.

Mrs. Crumble held up the envelope and dramatically ripped it open. She pulled out a letter written in shimmering, golden ink.

"Congratulations!" Mrs. Crumble read aloud. "You have won a once-in-a-lifetime trip... in a hot air balloon!"

The classroom erupted in cheers and gasps. A hot air balloon ride! The very idea of floating above the world, soaring through the clouds, sounded like the greatest adventure they could ever imagine.

"Who's going?" asked Max, hoping he'd be chosen.

"All of you!" Mrs. Crumble smiled. "Max, Lily, Finn, Ruby—you're the lucky winners. Tomorrow morning, you'll embark on an adventure through the skies."

The four friends couldn't believe their luck. They spent the entire night packing for their journey, barely able to sleep as they imagined what might lie ahead.

The next morning, they arrived at the Bumblebrook Meadows where, standing tall against the blue sky, was the biggest, most colorful hot air balloon they had ever seen. Its bright red and yellow stripes glistened in the sunlight, and the enormous basket below looked just big enough for the four of them.

The balloon's pilot, a jolly man named Captain Bouncer, greeted them with a wide grin. He wore goggles, a leather jacket, and an enormous scarf that flapped in the breeze. "Welcome aboard, adventurers!" he called, tipping his hat. "Are you ready for the ride of your lives?"

The children nodded eagerly as they climbed into the basket. With a great whoosh, the flames roared, filling the balloon with hot air, and soon they were lifting off the ground, leaving the town of Bumblebrook far below.

Up, up, and up they went, higher than the tallest trees, higher than the birds, until they were soaring among the clouds.

"This is amazing!" Lily shouted, her hair blowing wildly in the wind.

"I feel like I can touch the sky!" Finn added, reaching up as if he could grab a cloud.

Ruby leaned over the edge, her eyes sparkling. "Look! There's Bumblebrook—it looks so tiny from up here!"

Max, who had been a little nervous at first, grinned as the thrill of the adventure kicked in. "What do you think we'll see?"

As if in answer to his question, a kangaroo suddenly bounced out from behind a cloud.

"Yes, you heard that right—a kangaroo."

The kids stared in disbelief as the kangaroo hopped from one fluffy cloud to another, as if they were giant trampolines.

"That can't be real," Max whispered, rubbing his eyes.

But it was. The kangaroo stopped mid-bounce and looked directly at them. "G'day, mates!" it said with a cheerful wave. "Welcome to Cloudland! We love a good bounce up here. Care to join?"

The children blinked, speechless.

"Well, if you change your mind, just shout. The clouds are lovely and springy today!" The kangaroo gave one last bounce, disappearing into the misty white clouds.

"That... was bizarre," Lily said, still wide-eyed.

"Bizarre but awesome!" Ruby added, laughing.

Just as they thought things couldn't get stranger, a sudden rumble of laughter filled the air. The balloon wobbled as something enormous flew past—a dragon, but not just any dragon. This one was lounging on a giant sun lounger, wearing sunglasses and holding a tropical drink with a tiny umbrella.

"Nice day for a tan, huh?" the dragon called out, lazily flapping its wings to keep itself airborne.

The kids gawked in amazement.

"Um… shouldn't you be breathing fire and, you know, doing dragon things?" Finn asked.

The dragon chuckled, adjusting its sunglasses. "Nah, that's so last century. These days, I prefer relaxing in the sun. Fire breathing's too much work. Plus, have you ever tried keeping a flame going in this wind? Nearly impossible!"

The dragon let out a deep, satisfied sigh, and then drifted away, slowly vanishing behind a puffy white cloud.

Captain Bouncer laughed heartily. "Ah, you've met Drake! He's been up here for ages. Retired from all that knight-fighting nonsense."

The balloon floated peacefully for a while, but the surprises weren't over yet. Suddenly, a flock of sheep floated by, not on the ground, but in the sky. They were lounging on tiny personal clouds, munching on what appeared to be cotton candy. One of the sheep gave the kids a slow, lazy wave with its hoof.

"Cloud sheep," Ruby whispered. "I can't believe it."

As they sailed on, the friends encountered more and more strange characters. There was a rainbow-colored octopus hanging from the sky, painting the clouds with bright colors. A school of flying fish swam past them, glittering like stars. And at one point, they even spotted a penguin with a jetpack zooming around, leaving trails of ice behind.

But the most magical part of their journey came as they flew into the sunset. The sky turned shades of orange and pink, and the clouds glowed like lanterns. In the distance, they saw something glittering—a castle made entirely of stars. It floated in the night sky, its towers sparkling like diamonds.

"Look!" Max pointed. "That's where the King of the Clouds lives!"

The children gazed in awe as they drifted closer to the starry castle. They could hear the faint sound of music coming from inside, like a celestial symphony. Captain Bouncer steered the balloon gently around it, giving them a perfect view of the magical kingdom.

"I wish we could stay here forever," Ruby whispered, her heart full of wonder.

But soon, the sky began to darken, and it was time to return to Bumblebrook. The children sighed, reluctant to leave the magical world of the clouds. Slowly, the balloon descended, floating gently back down to earth.

When they finally touched down in the meadow, Mrs. Crumble was waiting for them. "How was it?" she asked, her eyes twinkling.

"It was... unbelievable," Max said, his voice full of awe.

"We met a cloud-bouncing kangaroo," Finn said.

"And a sunbathing dragon!" Lily added.

"And sheep in the sky!" Ruby exclaimed.

Mrs. Crumble smiled. "Ah, the wonders of the Great Balloon Adventure. I'm glad you all had fun."

As they walked back home, their feet now firmly on the ground, the children knew they had just experienced something truly magical. And though they were no longer floating among the clouds, they carried the joy and wonder of the adventure with them, knowing that the world was full of surprises just waiting to be discovered.

Das große Ballonabenteuer

Es war ein gewöhnlicher Freitagnachmittag in der kleinen Stadt Bumblebrook, als etwas Außergewöhnliches passierte. Vier Kinder—Max, Lily, Finn und Ruby—saßen im Unterricht, langweiligte sich zu Tode, als ihre Lehrerin, Frau Crumble, durch die Tür stürmte und einen goldenen Umschlag schwenkte.

„Kinder!" rief sie aus, ihr Gesicht leuchtete vor Aufregung. „Ihr werdet nicht glauben, was gerade angekommen ist!"

Max hob eine Augenbraue. Lily richtete sich auf und wurde neugierig. Finn, der immer tagträumte, blinzelte sich zurück in die Realität. Und Ruby, nun ja, Ruby stellte sich bereits etwas Großartiges vor.

Frau Crumble hielt den Umschlag hoch und riss ihn dramatisch auf. Sie zog einen Brief heraus, der in schimmernder, goldener Tinte geschrieben war.

„Herzlichen Glückwunsch!" las Frau Crumble laut vor. „Ihr habt eine einmalige Reise gewonnen... in einem Heißluftballon!"

Das Klassenzimmer brach in Jubel und Staunen aus. Eine Heißluftballonfahrt! Allein der Gedanke, über die Welt zu schweben, durch die Wolken zu fliegen, klang nach dem größten Abenteuer, das sie sich vorstellen konnten.

„Wer fährt mit?" fragte Max, in der Hoffnung, ausgewählt zu werden.

„Alle von euch!" Frau Crumble lächelte. „Max, Lily, Finn, Ruby—ihr seid die glücklichen Gewinner. Morgen früh werdet ihr zu einem Abenteuer durch den Himmel aufbrechen."

Die vier Freunde konnten ihr Glück nicht fassen. Sie verbrachten die ganze Nacht damit, für ihre Reise zu packen, kaum in der Lage zu schlafen, während sie sich vorstellten, was sie erwarten könnte.

———

AM NÄCHSTEN MORGEN kamen sie auf den Bumblebrook-Wiesen an, wo, hoch gegen den blauen Himmel, der größte und bunteste Heißluftballon stand, den sie je gesehen hatten. Seine leuchtend roten und gelben Streifen glitzerten in der Sonne, und der riesige Korb darunter sah gerade groß genug für die vier von ihnen aus.

Der Pilot des Ballons, ein fröhlicher Mann namens Captain Bouncer, begrüßte sie mit einem breiten Grinsen. Er trug eine Schutzbrille, eine Lederjacke und einen riesigen Schal, der im Wind flatterte. „Willkommen an Bord, Abenteurer!" rief er und neigte seinen Hut. „Seid ihr bereit für die Fahrt eures Lebens?"

Die Kinder nickten eifrig, als sie in den Korb kletterten. Mit einem großen Zischen brüllten die Flammen, füllten den Ballon mit heißer Luft, und bald hoben sie ab, ließen die Stadt Bumblebrook weit hinter sich.

Hoch, hoch und immer höher ging es, höher als die höchsten Bäume, höher als die Vögel, bis sie zwischen den Wolken schwebten.

„Das ist erstaunlich!" rief Lily, während ihr Haar wild im Wind wehte.

„Ich fühle mich, als könnte ich den Himmel berühren!" fügte Finn hinzu und streckte die Arme aus, als könnte er eine Wolke greifen.

Ruby lehnte sich über den Rand, ihre Augen funkelten. „Schau! Da ist Bumblebrook—von hier oben sieht es so winzig aus!"

Max, der anfangs ein wenig nervös gewesen war, grinste, als das Abenteuergefühl einsetzte. „Was denkt ihr, werden wir sehen?"

Als ob in Antwort auf seine Frage, sprang plötzlich ein Känguru hinter einer Wolke hervor.

„Ja, du hast richtig gehört—ein Känguru."

Die Kinder starrten ungläubig, als das Känguru von einer flauschigen Wolke zur anderen hüpfte, als wären sie riesige Trampoline.

„Das kann nicht echt sein," flüsterte Max und rieb sich die Augen.

Aber es war echt. Das Känguru hielt mitten im Sprung an und schaute direkt zu ihnen. „G'day, mates!" sagte es mit einem fröhlichen Winken. „Willkommen im Wolkenland! Wir lieben ein gutes Hüpfen hier oben. Wollt ihr mitmachen?"

Die Kinder blinzelten, sprachlos.

„Nun, wenn ihr eure Meinung ändert, ruft einfach. Die Wolken sind heute schön und elastisch!" Das Känguru machte einen letzten Sprung und verschwand in den nebligen, weißen Wolken.

„Das... war bizarr," sagte Lily, immer noch mit großen Augen.

„Bizarre, aber großartig!" fügte Ruby lachend hinzu.

Gerade als sie dachten, es könnte nicht seltsamer werden, erfüllte ein plötzliches Gelächter die Luft. Der Ballon wackelte, als etwas Enormes vorbeiflog—ein Drache, aber nicht irgendein Drache. Dieser lag auf einer riesigen Sonnenliege, trug eine Sonnenbrille und hielt ein tropisches Getränk mit einem kleinen Regenschirm.

„Schöner Tag zum Bräunen, was?" rief der Drache und schlug faul mit den Flügeln, um in der Luft zu bleiben.

Die Kinder starrten verblüfft.

„Ähm... solltest du nicht Feuer speien und, weißt du, Drachen-Dinge tun?" fragte Finn.

Der Drache kicherte, während er seine Sonnenbrille zurechtrückte. „Nein, das ist so letzte Jahrhundert. Heutzutage entspanne ich lieber in der Sonne. Feuer speien ist zu viel Arbeit. Und hast du schon mal versucht, eine Flamme in diesem Wind am Laufen zu halten? Fast unmöglich!"

Der Drache ließ einen tiefen, zufriedenen Seufzer los und driftete dann davon, verschwand langsam hinter einer fluffigen weißen Wolke.

Captain Bouncer lachte herzhaft. „Ah, ihr habt Drake getroffen! Er ist schon seit Ewigkeiten hier oben. Hat sich von all dem Ritterkämpfen zurückgezogen."

Der Ballon schwebte eine Weile friedlich, aber die Überraschungen waren noch nicht vorbei. Plötzlich schwebte eine Herde Schafe vorbei, nicht auf dem Boden, sondern am Himmel. Sie lagen auf kleinen persönlichen Wolken und kauten auf dem, was wie Zuckerwatte aussah. Eines der Schafe winkte den Kindern langsam und faul mit seiner Huf.

„Wolkenschafe," flüsterte Ruby. „Ich kann es nicht fassen."

Während sie weitersegelten, trafen die Freunde immer mehr seltsame Figuren. Da war ein regenbogenfarbener Oktopus, der am Himmel hing und die Wolken mit hellen Farben malte. Ein Schwarm fliegender Fische schwamm an ihnen vorbei, glitzernd wie Sterne. Und irgendwann sahen sie sogar einen Pinguin mit einem Jetpack, der herumzoomte und Eisstreifen hinterließ.

Aber der magischste Teil ihrer Reise kam, als sie in den Sonnenuntergang flogen. Der Himmel wurde orange und rosa, und die Wolken leuchteten wie Laternen. In der Ferne sahen sie etwas Glitzerndes—ein Schloss, das ganz aus Sternen bestand. Es schwebte am Nachthimmel, seine Türme funkelten wie Diamanten.

„Schaut!" Max deutete. „Dort wohnt der König der Wolken!"

Die Kinder starrten voller Ehrfurcht, als sie näher an das sternenklare Schloss drifteten. Sie konnten die leisen Klänge von Musik hören, die von innen kamen, wie eine himmlische Symphonie. Captain Bouncer steuerte den Ballon sanft darum herum, sodass sie einen perfekten Blick auf das magische Königreich hatten.

„Ich wünschte, wir könnten für immer hier bleiben," flüsterte Ruby, ihr Herz voller Staunen.

Aber bald begann der Himmel sich zu verdunkeln, und es war Zeit, nach Bumblebrook zurückzukehren. Die Kinder seufzten, widerwillig, die magische Welt der Wolken zu verlassen. Langsam sank der Ballon und schwebte sanft zurück zur Erde.

Als sie schließlich auf der Wiese landeten, wartete Frau Crumble auf sie. „Wie war es?" fragte sie, ihre Augen funkelnd.

„Es war... unglaublich," sagte Max, seine Stimme voller Ehrfurcht.

„Wir haben ein wolkenhüpfendes Känguru getroffen," sagte Finn.

„Und einen sonnenbadenden Drachen!" fügte Lily hinzu.

„Und Schafe im Himmel!" rief Ruby aus.

Frau Crumble lächelte. „Ah, die Wunder des großen Ballonabenteuers. Ich freue mich, dass ihr alle Spaß hattet."

Als sie zurück nach Hause gingen, ihre Füße fest auf dem Boden, wussten die Kinder, dass sie gerade etwas wahrhaft Magisches erlebt hatten. Und obwohl sie nicht mehr zwischen den Wolken schwebten, trugen sie die Freude und das Staunen des Abenteuers mit sich, in dem Wissen, dass die Welt voller Überraschungen war, die nur darauf warteten, entdeckt zu werden.